W9-DBV-037

LAKE CLASSICS

*Great Short Stories
from Around the World I*

Guy de
MAUPASSANT

Stories retold by Prescott Hill
Illustrated by James McConnell

LAKE EDUCATION
Belmont, California

LAKE CLASSICS

Great American Short Stories I

Washington Irving, Nathaniel Hawthorne, Mark Twain, Bret Harte, Edgar Allan Poe, Kate Chopin, Willa Cather, Sarah Orne Jewett, Sherwood Anderson, Charles W. Chesnutt

Great American Short Stories II

Herman Melville, Stephen Crane, Ambrose Bierce, Jack London, Edith Wharton, Charlotte Perkins Gilman, Frank R. Stockton, Hamlin Garland, O. Henry, Richard Harding Davis

Great British and Irish Short Stories I

Arthur Conan Doyle, Saki (H. H. Munro), Rudyard Kipling, Katherine Mansfield, Thomas Hardy, E. M. Forster, Robert Louis Stevenson, H. G. Wells, John Galsworthy, James Joyce

Great Short Stories from Around the World I

Guy de Maupassant, Anton Chekhov, Leo Tolstoy, Selma Lagerlöf, Alphonse Daudet, Mori Ogwai, Leopoldo Alas, Rabindranath Tagore, Fyodor Dostoevsky, Honoré de Balzac

Cover and Text Designer: Diann Abbott

Library of Congress Catalog Number: 94-075350
ISBN 1-56103-039-2
Printed in the United States of America
1 9 8 7 6 5 4 3 2

CONTENTS

🎋 Lake Classic Short Stories 🎋

"The universe is made of stories, not atoms."
　　　—Muriel Rukeyser

"The story's about you."
　　　—Horace

Everyone loves a good story. It is hard to think of a friendlier introduction to classic literature. For one thing, short stories are *short*—quick to get into and easy to finish. Of all the literary forms, the short story is the least intimidating and the most approachable.

Great literature is an important part of our human heritage. In the belief that this heritage belongs to everyone, *Lake Classic Short Stories* are adapted for today's readers. Lengthy sentences and paragraphs are shortened. Archaic words are replaced. Modern punctuation and spellings are used. Many of the longer stories are abridged. In all the stories,

5

painstaking care has been taken to preserve the author's unique voice.

Lake Classic Short Stories have something for everyone. The hundreds of stories in the collection cover a broad terrain of themes, story types, and styles. Literary merit was a deciding factor in story selection. But no story was included unless it was as enjoyable as it was instructive. And special priority was given to stories that shine light on the human condition.

Each book in the *Lake Classic Short Stories* is devoted to the work of a single author. Little-known stories of merit are included with famous old favorites. Taken as a whole, the collected authors and stories make up a rich and diverse sampler of the story-teller's art.

Lake Classic Short Stories guarantee a great reading experience. Readers who look for common interests, concerns, and experiences are sure to find them. Readers who bring their own gifts of perception and appreciation to the stories will be doubly rewarded.

❦ Guy de Maupassant ❦
(1850–1893)

About the Author

Guy de Maupassant was born near Dieppe, France. Handsome and well-built, he was a fine athlete in his youth. One of his favorite sports was rowing on the River Seine.

The great French author Gustav Flaubert happened to be a friend of Maupassant's mother. So it was only by chance that the carefree young athlete was introduced to the great master. From the first, Maupassant was determined to follow in Flaubert's footsteps.

At first Flaubert saw no talent in the eager young man. Only as a favor did he agree to take on Maupassant as a student. What followed was a rigorous apprenticeship that lasted seven years.

It turned out that Maupassant had talents for short fiction that his famous teacher lacked. He could write a dozen stories while Flaubert was writing one. Not bound by formal rules of style, Maupassant wrote freely. In just ten years he published nearly 300 short stories of every variety. During the same period, he wrote plays, poetry, travel books, and six novels.

Maupassant's colorful and varied short stories were very popular in the magazines of his day. The income from his huge literary output guaranteed his financial security. But unfortunately, his appetite for wild living quickly went out of control. When his capacity for work fell off, he looked for relief in drugs. He was only 43 when he died in an insane asylum.

Some think that Maupassant has no equal in the short story form. Others disagree. But no one doubts the influence of his work on the generations of writers that came after him.

The Necklace

Have you ever misplaced
something valuable? In this
famous story, a poor woman
loses a borrowed necklace.
What will she have to give
up to replace it?

"I THINK I HAVE JUST THE THING FOR YOU!"

The Necklace

Matilda Loisel did not come from a rich family. She was pretty and smart, but that was not enough for her. Those things didn't make up for the one thing she wanted most. They could not take the place of a rich husband.

The man she did marry was a clerk by the name of Robert Loisel. He worked for the School Department. Although his salary was not large, his job was a good one. The important thing was, it was steady work. The Loisels were not rich, but they were not poor either. They had a small house in a pleasant part of the city. They had clothes on their backs. They had enough to eat. They even had a cook. True, she was not a fancy cook, but she prepared good, healthy meals. Mr. Loisel was a kind man. He loved Matilda and treated her well. He was very happy with their life together.

But she was not happy. She thought she should have better things. She wanted a bigger house. She wanted to wear better clothes.

She wanted to eat fancy foods and to meet fancy people. Most of her friends thought she had a nice house. It was big enough for her and Robert. It was cool in the hot days of summer. It was warm when the snows of winter came.

That was not enough for her. She wanted to live in a house with many grand rooms. She wanted a house where she could hold large parties. She wanted to have servants. She wanted the kind of cook that rich people had. Robert loved the food their cook served. Matilda did not. He was pleased to have a good fish soup for dinner. A nice chicken dinner always made him happy. He did not want anything more than good, plain food. But Matilda did. She wanted to eat lobster. She wanted fancy cakes. She wanted to eat her food off gold dishes.

Matilda's clothes were plain, but in good shape. They were clean and comfortable and had no holes in them. Robert thought they looked fine on her. She did not. She wanted to dress like a rich woman. She wanted to wear fancy hats. She wanted to wear silk dresses. She wanted pretty jewels.

Matilda was sure she could be happy if she only had such things. She thought all rich people were happy. Although she and Robert were not poor, they were not really rich. She wanted to be rich! Matilda's friend Ann was rich. The two women had been friends for many years. They had gone to school together. After they finished school, they had stayed in touch. Matilda visited Ann every two weeks or so.

Matilda was always sad after these visits. She always wished she could trade places with Ann. The differences in their lives bothered Matilda. Ann had so many good things and she herself had so few. It just was not fair!

One night Robert came home from work early. He had a big smile on his face. "Look," he said, handing her an envelope. She took out the letter and read it. It was an invitation to a party from the head of the School Department. When Matilda finished reading it, she threw it on the table. Robert was surprised.

"My dear," he said, "whatever is the matter? Don't you want to go the party? We will visit my employer's house for the first time. It is a great honor."

Matilda made a face. "It may be an honor for you," she said. "It will not be an honor for me."

Robert took her hands in his. He could see a tear rolling down her cheek. "Please, my dear," he said, "do not look so sad!"

"But I *am* sad," she said. "What do you think I should wear to a party like that?"

Robert looked surprised once more. "Why, you can wear your pretty red dress," he said. "I think it looks very nice on you."

More tears fell from her eyes. "No," she said. "I will not wear that dress. It is old, and it is cheap. The rich people will laugh at me. They will think I am some poor woman who was let into the party by mistake."

"But my dear—" Robert started to say.

"Enough!" Matilda shouted. "Say no more. I don't have the right kind of dress for such a party. I can't go. I *won't* go."

Robert was very upset. He had hoped the invitation would make her happy. It had not. His wife was sadder than he had ever seen her before.

Then he got an idea. "Wait," he said, "think about this. Let us get you a new dress. We will have a nice one made. How would that be?"

She did think about it. If he gave her enough money, she could get just the kind of dress she wanted. But it had to be *enough*. She wouldn't go to the party in anything but a *very* fancy dress.

"Well," she said, "perhaps I would go if I had the right dress."

Robert smiled.

"But it will cost quite a bit," she said.

Robert made a face. "How much do you think it will cost?"

She thought quickly. She didn't want to ask for too much. But then again, she did not want to ask for too little. Finally she said, "I think I could get one made for $300."

Robert's face turned a little pale. He had saved almost $300 to buy himself a new gun. Hunting was his favorite sport. But the gun he had was getting old. He didn't think it would last much longer. He saw that he would have to forget the new gun for now. The dress was more important. His employer would be angry at him if he didn't bring his wife to the party. And she wouldn't go to the party without a new dress. So, there was nothing else for him to do.

"Well, Matilda," he said, "I will give you $300. But try to get a very pretty dress for the money. We won't be able to get another for a long time."

* * * *

Two days before the party, Matilda seemed sad. Robert didn't know what was the matter with her. She had her new dress, and it was a very fancy one. What could be the trouble? Finally, he said, "Matilda, you have been acting strangely all day. Is something bothering you?"

At first she said nothing. Then once again the tears began to fall. Finally she answered. "Yes, something is bothering me. I am very sad because I don't have any jewels to wear to the party. All the people there will think I am poor. I don't think I could stand that. Perhaps I should stay home after all."

"Cheer up," Robert said. "You can wear some fresh flowers. They always look so lovely on you. For $10 or so we can get some nice roses."

"No!" she said. "All the rich ladies will

laugh at me behind my back."

Then Robert cried out, "Wait! I have an idea. Go and see your good friend Ann. She has beautiful jewels. She will let you wear some to the party if you ask her."

A big smile came to Matilda's face. "That is true," she said. "What a good idea! I will visit her tomorrow and ask to borrow some jewels."

The next day she went to see Ann. When she told her friend about the party, Ann was happy for her. "Of course you can borrow some jewels," she said. Ann went to her closet and got down her large jewel case. She opened it and said, "Pick whatever you want."

Matilda's eyes got bright. She took a gold bracelet from the case and tried it on. It was beautiful, but not quite what she wanted. Then she tried on a diamond ring. It was beautiful, too, but not exactly what she wanted. She tried several other things, but none seemed right. At last, she said, "Ann, do you have *anything* else?"

Ann thought for a moment. Then she smiled. "I think I have just the thing for you!" She went into the closet again and came out with a black satin box. She opened it and took out a beautiful necklace of diamonds. Matilda took the necklace and put it on. When she looked in the mirror, her heart began to beat faster. It was the most beautiful necklace she had ever seen! Wearing it made her look more beautiful herself. And it made her *feel* beautiful.

"Could I borrow this?" she asked Ann. "It's the only thing I will need."

"Why, yes," Ann said, "certainly."

Matilda gave her friend a big hug. "Thank you so much," she said. Then she headed home with the necklace, smiling all the way.

* * * *

At last the night of the party came. Matilda looked beautiful indeed. All the people there wanted to talk with her. All the men wanted to dance with her. Robert's employer was very happy she had come. He patted Robert on the back. "You have a beautiful wife," he said. "You must bring her to my next party." Matilda was happier than she had ever been before. She no longer felt like a poor person. In fact, she felt like the richest woman in the world.

In the early hours of the morning, she and Robert took a cab home. She had danced all night and was dead tired, but happy. What a party it had been! When she got home she went right to the mirror. She wanted one last look at herself.

She stood before the mirror and took off her coat. Then she let out a cry. Her neck was bare. The necklace was missing!

"What is the matter?" Robert asked.

"I have—I have lost the necklace."

"What?" he said. He could not believe it. How could it have gotten lost?

They looked in the pockets of the coat, but it was not there. They looked in the folds of her dress. They looked on the floor. They looked on the steps outside the house. It was nowhere to be found.

"It must be in the cab," Matilda said.

"Did you get the number of the cab?" Robert asked.

"No," she said. "Did you?"

He shook his head. "No," he said.

They looked at each other, their eyes full of sadness.

"What will we do?" Matilda cried.

"I will check with the cab company later in the day," Robert said. "Now we must get to bed. I have to leave for work in a few hours. I need what little sleep I can get."

When he did check with the cab company, he got bad news. No one there had found the necklace. Then he checked with the police department. Again, he got bad news. No one had turned in the necklace to the police. He didn't give up. That same day he put an ad in the newspaper. He offered a reward to anyone who found the necklace.

Matilda waited at home. When Robert

returned that night, she rushed to meet him at the door.

"Did you find it?" she said.

Robert shook his head. "No," he said, "but there is still hope. Maybe someone will answer my newspaper ad."

A tear rolled down Matilda's cheek. "What about Ann?" she said. "I told her I would return the necklace after the party."

Robert thought for a moment. Then he said, "I know what we'll do. Write to her and say the clasp of the necklace broke. Tell her we are having it fixed. That will give us a little more time." Matilda wrote the letter and mailed it that night.

By the end of the week they had lost all hope. No one had turned in the necklace to the police. No one had answered the ad in the newspaper.

Just one week had passed, but Robert looked five years older.

"Well," he told Matilda, "we have no choice. We must buy a new necklace to replace the lost one."

She nodded, a downcast look on her face. She knew what he said was true. The next day they went looking for a necklace. They went from store to store without luck. They saw many necklaces, but none that looked like the lost one.

Finally, they went to a small store on the edge of town. There in the jeweler's window they saw the necklace they wanted. It looked very much like the lost one.

The store owner said it was worth $50,000.

Matilda and Robert both turned pale.

"But," the store owner said, "I will sell it for less."

A bit of hope showed in Robert's face.

"I will sell it to you for only $45,000," the man said.

"All right," Robert said, "but I don't have the money just now. I will bring it to you tomorrow."

"Fine," the jeweler said. "But make sure you are here by noon. If not, I might have to sell it to someone else."

Robert had just $18,000 his father had left him in his will. His only hope was to borrow the rest from friends. That was not an easy job. No one he knew could lend him the whole $27,000. So he borrowed $3,000 from one person. Another loaned him $2,000. Some people could lend him only $100 or $200. He promised them all he would pay them back with interest. At last he got the $45,000 he needed to buy the necklace.

When Matilda returned the necklace, Ann seemed cross. "You should have brought it back sooner," she said. "What if I needed to wear it?" Matilda did not dare say anything. Her only hope was that Ann would not see that it was a different necklace. Ann didn't seem to notice. She put the sparkling necklace away in her closet without saying anything more.

From then on, life grew hard for Robert and Matilda. Their frightful debt took all their money. They could not afford to live the way they once had. They no longer had enough money to pay a cook. And they could no longer hire a lady to help Matilda clean house.

For the first time in her life, Matilda had to find a job. Because she had never worked before, it was not easy to find one. At last she found work washing dishes and scrubbing floors at a hotel. It tired her out. After work, she had to take care of the house by herself. Robert had no time to help her with the cleaning and cooking. He had been forced to take a night job to pay off the loans. They had little time together, for they both worked weekends, too.

At the end of 10 years, they had finally paid off all the loans. But it had cost them much more than money. They both looked much, much older than they really were. The years of hard work had worn them down.

Robert walked with his head bent down. He wore thick glasses now. Ten years of bookkeeping from dawn to dark had strained his eyes. Matilda was no longer a pretty woman. Her hands were red from washing dishes. There were lines on her face from lack of sleep. Her clothes were patched and baggy. The poor woman's back was bent from scrubbing floors. Her hair was no longer beautiful. It had lost its pretty yellow color. Now it looked as gray and as dirty as dishwater.

Matilda no longer smiled when Robert came home. She was too tired to be cheerful. And so it was with him also. The years of hard work had taken the joy from his life.

Matilda often remembered how their life had once been. When she had these thoughts, tears trickled from her eyes. The necklace had changed everything. Such a small thing to have caused such great sadness!

One day in the park Matilda saw her old friend Ann. They had not seen each other for many years. The last time, in fact, was the day Matilda returned the necklace.

"Hello, Ann," she said.

Ann turned and looked at her. "I don't think I know you," she said to Matilda.

"It is I, Matilda."

Ann could not believe it at first. She herself still looked young and pretty. But Matilda had changed so much! She did not look like the same woman.

Matilda could see the look of shock on her old friend's face. She said, "I know I look old and worn, Ann—but it is all because of you."

"Because of *me*?" Ann gasped. "How could that be?"

"Do you remember the necklace I borrowed?" Matilda said.

"Yes, very well," Ann said.

"Well, I lost it."

"That can't be so. You returned it to me," Ann said.

"No," Matilda said. "I returned a diamond necklace just like it. But I lost the one you loaned me. It has taken Robert and me ten years to pay for it. It was very hard for us. But it is finished, and I no longer have to worry about it."

A funny look came to Ann's face. "You say you bought a diamond necklace to replace mine?"

"Yes," Matilda said. "It was just like yours."

Ann stepped toward her old friend and hugged her. "Oh! my poor Matilda!" she said. "The diamonds in the necklace I loaned you were not real. They were not worth more than $20!"

The Umbrella

Do you know anyone who's downright *stingy*? In this amusing story, a husband takes a stand against his penny-pinching wife. But can *anything* make her change her ways?

PEOPLE AT WORK MADE JOKES ABOUT HIS UMBRELLA.
HE TOLD HIS WIFE HE NEEDED A NEW ONE.

The Umbrella

Madame Oreille knew the value of money better than she knew anything else. She and her husband were not poor. They lived in a nice house. They even had enough money to hire a cook.

But she watched every cent carefully. She spent all her time worrying about waste. She made sure the cook didn't waste so much as a penny. Every morning the cook went shopping for the day's food. When she got back, Madame Oreille checked the list twice. She had to make sure the cook didn't pay too much for anything.

Madame Oreille took charge of all the money in the house. She even shopped for her husband's clothes. She and her husband had no children. That saved money. And she didn't allow him to buy many things for himself. That too saved money. Spending any money at all tore at her heartstrings. If she had to buy some small thing—no matter how necessary—she slept badly that night.

Her husband thought she worried too much about money. He often said, "Why are you so careful with money? We don't need to save so much. We have no children to leave it to. And we can't take it with us when we die."

"Maybe not," she said. "But we don't know what may happen. It is better to have too much money than too little."

Madame Oreille was a small woman, about 40 years old. She was a very neat and tidy person. She walked with quick steps. Sometimes she had a bad temper. Her husband wished she would not act so cross and crabby. But most of all he wished she would let him have a little more money to spend. She watched his spending as carefully as she watched the cook's.

Oreille worked harder than he needed to. Since he had worked hard and spent little for so many years, they had saved a lot of money. For a long time he had wanted to leave his job. But his wife would not let him. She said they needed more money. She thought they needed all the money they could get!

The other clerks at Oreille's office often laughed at him. Even though he had plenty of money, he did not dress well. His clothes were old and faded. One of his shoes had a hole in the bottom. His umbrella was full of holes. The people at work had made many rude jokes about his umbrella.

That seemed to bother him more than anything.

At last he could stand it no longer. He told his wife he must have a new umbrella. He demanded that she get him a good silk one—and spend plenty of money for it, too.

Finally, she did buy him one. But it was cheap. It was the cheapest umbrella she could find. It only cost a few dollars— and it looked it. When he took it to work, everybody joked about it.

That made Oreille very angry. He told his wife he wanted a good umbrella this time. "I told you I wanted a silk one. No more of that cheap stuff. I want you to spend at least $30 for it!"

She made a face. That was too much money! But she saw how angry her husband was. She guessed she would have to do as he asked.

The next day she went to the store to find another umbrella. There were many to choose from. She was tempted to buy another cheap one.

That was an idea—she could buy it for a few dollars and then say it cost a lot! But she decided not to. It would not fool her husband. He would want to see the bill. Then he would get angry at her all over again.

At last she found just the umbrella she wanted. It was supposed to cost $30. But today it was on sale. She got it for $25. She kept the $5 she had saved for herself. Her husband had demanded a $30 umbrella. Well, that's what he was getting. So what if she only had to pay $25 for it?

She gave the umbrella to her husband that night. She was not happy about it. It seemed like such a waste of money. Her face got red when she gave it to him. That's how angry she was.

"This should last for five years," she said. "You had better take care of it!"

Her husband was pleased. At last he had a fine looking umbrella. It was made of real silk. It didn't have any holes in it. It didn't look cheap like the other one she had bought him.

The next day he took it to work. All the people in the office thought it looked great. They wouldn't make jokes about his umbrella any longer.

That night when he came home, his wife was waiting. She took the umbrella from him. "Have you been careful with this?" she said. "It cost a lot of money, you know."

"Of course I was careful," he said.

But when she opened it, she let out a shout. "What is this? Look!"

She pointed to a hole in the silk covering. It was the size of a dime. It looked like a cigarette had burned it.

"What are you talking about?" he said.

Her face was getting red. "This!" she said, rushing toward him. She held the umbrella up to his face. "You have ruined it the very first day!"

He backed away from her. "I don't know where the hole came from," he insisted.

"You were playing tricks with it!" she shouted. "You had to show it off!"

"I only opened it once," he said. "I wanted everyone to see how nice it was."

"Well, see what you have done," she said. "You have ruined the umbrella. And after all the good money I spent on it! Are you trying to ruin us?"

"Do you think you can fix it?" he asked meekly.

"Maybe," she said, still angry. "I will see what I can do."

She cut a piece from the old, cheap umbrella. She sewed it over the hole in the new one. It was a different color. He didn't like the way it looked, but he didn't dare complain.

The next night when he came home from work, she was waiting.

"Let's see that," she said. She took the umbrella from him and opened it.

"Oh, no!" she shouted. "Look at that!"

Somebody must have dropped hot ashes on it. It was covered with little holes. There were far too many to fix. This time the umbrella was really ruined.

Oreille and his wife looked at each other without saying a word.

At last Madame Oreille could keep quiet no longer. Her face was getting very red. "You fool!" she shouted. "You did it on purpose."

Her husband said nothing.

"Well," she said, "that is that. I will not get you another one."

Just then they heard a bell ring. Oreille went to the front door to see who was there. It was a friend, just stopping by to say hello.

As soon as the man came inside, Madame Oreille started to talk.

She showed him the umbrella. "See how my husband has ruined it?" she said. "It cost a lot of money. Now he will have to do without an umbrella."

"Well," the friend said, "that will cost even more money."

"How can that be?" Madame Oreille asked.

"If it rains," the friend said, "your husband will need an umbrella. Without one, his clothes will get wet. Before long they will be ruined. And clothes cost a lot more than an umbrella."

"Yes, that is true," Madame Oreille thought to herself. But it didn't make her happy.

"All right," she said. "He will just have to use the old umbrella then."

"No!" Oreille shouted. "I will not use that cheap, old thing. I will quit my job before I take it to the office again."

Madame Oreille said nothing. But her face was getting very red.

"Wait," the friend said. "There is a way out of this. You can have the burned umbrella covered in new silk. It will not cost as much as a new umbrella. And it will still look very nice."

"That will cost at least $10," Madame Oreille said. "Add that to the $25 the umbrella cost in the first place and you have $35. That is way too much to pay for an umbrella!"

"Well," the friend said, "what about fire insurance?"

"Fire insurance?" Oreille said.

"Yes," the friend said. "You have fire insurance for your house, don't you?"

"Yes, of course we do," Oreille said. "Everybody who owns a house has fire insurance."

"Then everything is fine," the friend said. "The insurance company will pay if the fire was in your house."

"Right you are," said Madame Oreille. She smiled and looked at her husband. "Tomorrow," she said, "you must go to the insurance company. Show them the burned umbrella and make them pay for a new one."

"No!" Oreille shouted. "I will not do it! There was no fire in this house. I will not say there was."

He made a face. "Beside that, it is not that much money. We are only talking about $25."

Madame Oreille gave her husband an angry look. *"Only?"* she said.

And that was the last thing she said to him all night.

The next day Oreille went to work without an umbrella. He was lucky. It didn't rain. At home, Madame Oreille felt sad. All she could think of was the money they had spent. It had all gone for nothing. She tried to stop thinking about it. But that didn't help. Again and again the thought came back.

Then she began to think about the insurance. Would the insurance company pay? It would make her so happy if they did. But she was afraid. How could she face the people in the insurance office? She would have to tell them the fire was in her house. Would they believe her? Would she get in trouble?

Finally, she made up her mind.

"I will go," she told herself. "I will see what will happen."

But first she had to get the umbrella ready. She wanted it to look really bad. It was ruined, all right. It had all those little holes in it. But it had to look like it had been in a fire. She lit a match and held it against the umbrella. It burned a big hole in the silk.

"That should fool them," she said.

Then she put the umbrella in a bag and left the house.

She walked very fast. Soon she was near the insurance company. But then she began to get scared again. What if they found out her story was not true? What would they say to her? Would they call the police? Her heart began to beat faster. She stood outside the building, thinking.

At last she made up her mind. "I have to do it," she thought. "I might as well do it now rather than later."

She opened the door to the insurance company and walked into a very big room. There were desks everywhere. The people who sat behind the desks all seemed busy.

For a moment she just stood there, her heart beating faster and faster. Then she heard a voice.

"Can I help you?" a man said to her.

"Yes," she said in a small voice. She could feel herself shaking. "There has been a fire at my house. It burned something that cost a lot. Where do I go to get my money?"

He pointed to a door. "They take care of such things in there."

"Thank you," she said.

She headed for the door. Now she was feeling even more scared. She stopped outside the door. For a second, she thought of turning back. Then she thought about the $25. That made her feel a little braver. She knocked on the door.

"Come in," a deep voice said.

She opened the door and walked into another room. It was almost as big as the first one. But there were only two desks in it. The man sitting behind the desk near the door looked at her. "Good morning, Madame. What can I do for you?" he asked. He was the one who had told her to come in. His deep voice scared Madame Oreille.

"I have come—" she said, and then stopped.

"Yes?" the man said.

"I have come about a fire," she said.

"I see," the man said. "Please sit down." He pointed to a chair next to his desk. "Just let me finish some business." Then he turned to the man behind the other desk. "As I was saying, those people want too much."

The second man nodded his head. "You're right," he said. "Five million dollars *is* too much."

"We will offer them four million dollars," the first man said. "Not a penny more."

"I agree," the second man said. "I will go and tell them that." He got up from his chair and left the room.

The first man looked at Madame Oreille. "Now," he said, "how can I help you?"

She opened her mouth and said, "I—" But she could say no more than that.

The man gave her a funny look. "Go on," he said. "What are you trying to say?"

Madame Oreille could feel her heart beating faster. She opened her mouth again. "I have come about this," she said. She showed him the paper bag.

"What is it?" he asked.

"An umbrella," she said. She took it out of the bag and held it in front of him.

"Look!" she said, opening it up.

"Well," he said, "it surely is in bad shape."

"Do you know how much it cost me?" she asked.

"I have no idea," the man said.

She thought for a moment before speaking. She had paid $25 for the umbrella. But that was because it was on sale. There was no need to tell him that.

"Well," she said, "It cost me $30!"

"Really!" the man said. "As much as that?"

"Yes," she said. "And now look at it." She handed it to him.

"It *is* in very bad shape," he said. "But what do you want me to do about it?"

She opened her mouth to speak, but said nothing. Then it came to her. She must tell him about the insurance policy.

"We have fire insurance from your company," she said.

"I see," he said. "But what does that have to do with this?" He held the umbrella up and looked at it again.

"I want you to fix it," she said.

"But we don't do that sort of thing," he said. "We are an insurance company. We don't sell umbrellas. And we don't fix them."

"I know you don't fix them," she said. "I want you to pay me the cost of getting it fixed."

The man gave her a funny look. "Pay for getting an umbrella fixed? Madame Oreille, we don't take care of little things like that. We are a big company. We pay when there are big fires. We don't pay for every little thing that might get burned."

Madame Oreille's face began to get red. "That's not fair!" she shouted. "Last year we had a big fire and we didn't ask you to pay."

He gave her another funny look.

"It was in our kitchen," she said. "It cost us a thousand dollars to repair the damage."

The man guessed she was telling a lie. He smiled. "That seems odd," he said. "When you had a big fire, you didn't ask for money. Now you want us to pay for an umbrella?"

"There is nothing odd about it," Madame Oreille insisted. "The thousand dollars came out of my husband's pocket. This $30 came out of mine!"

"I see," the man said.

What he saw was that she was wasting his time. He guessed the best thing would be to pay her. It would be the only way to get rid of her.

He looked at the umbrella again. "Please tell me how this happened," he said.

She smiled. Now they were getting somewhere. In fact, she felt she had won.

"Let me see," she said, starting to make up a story. "It happened in the kitchen. The umbrella was on a shelf near the stove."

"You keep your umbrella in the kitchen?" the man asked.

"Not always," she said. "But I did last

night." Then she added, "We had visitors. There was no room anywhere else."

The man turned his head to hide his smile. This woman was a very good liar!

"And then what happened?" he asked.

"And then—" she said. "And then the cat must have knocked the umbrella onto the stove."

"I see," the man said.

"Yes, that was it," she said. "When I heard the sound, I ran to the kitchen. But the umbrella was on fire."

By now the man was growing tired of her lies. "How much will it cost to fix the umbrella?"

She did not answer at first. She was not sure how much she should ask for. Would they pay for a new umbrella? Or would they just pay to have this one fixed?

At last she said, "Why don't you get it fixed? I will leave it with you."

"Oh, no," he said. "Just tell me how much it will cost."

"Well—let me see," she said. She thought for a minute. The she said, "Sir,

I don't want to make any money out of this. I just want to get back what was lost. I will take it to a store and have a new silk cover put on it. Then I will bring the bill to you. Will that suit you?"

"Yes," he said. He was glad to be rid of her. "Have it fixed and send us the bill."

"Thank you," she said. She turned and hurried from the room. She didn't want to give him time to change his mind.

Outside the insurance company, she stopped to catch her breath. A big smile came to her face. Her plan had worked! She headed across town. She knew of a first-class shop that could fix her umbrella.

When she got there she smiled again. It was a very fancy shop. She had never been inside it before. She had always thought things cost too much there. Now, she walked in as though she were used to such places.

She told the man at the counter, "I want this umbrella fixed. Use the very best silk you have."

The man took the umbrella from her.

He held it up and looked at it closely. "Our best silk isn't cheap," he said. "You are talking about a lot of money."

Madame Oreille laughed. "What do I care?" she said. "I never mind how much a thing costs."

The Specter

Would you do a favor for an unlucky friend? In this story a simple errand turns into a horrifying experience. And the friend who asked the favor seems to have disappeared. . . .

I HAVE NEVER BELIEVED IN GHOSTS. STILL, MY HANDS
WERE SHAKING AND I COULD NOT SPEAK.

The Specter

I am an old man now, a few months older than 82 years. In my life I have seen many strange things. The strangest of all happened 56 years ago in a small French town. Not a month goes by that I do not dream about it. When I have those dreams, I wake up filled with an old fear.

On that day so many years ago, I felt that fear for the first time. It still haunts me. I can feel it when I hear a sudden noise. I can feel it when I see shapes hidden in the shadows. I must tell you the truth. Because of what happened, I am afraid of the dark!

I have never told a single soul what happened back then. But now I will tell you. I will not try to explain why it happened. I will only give you the facts.

On that day, I was living near the town of Rouen. I had a small house not far from the sea. As I was taking a walk on the beach one day, I met an old friend. What a surprise it was! I had not seen him for more than five years. When we were boys, though, he had been my best friend. He seemed to have grown old very quickly. His hair was white, and he walked bent over like an old man. How could that be? I knew for a fact that we were both only 26 years old.

He saw the look on my face.

"I know I look old," he said, "but there is a reason. Something awful happened to me a few years ago. It was such a shock that it turned me into an old man."

"I see that," I said.

"Let me tell you what happened," he said. "I fell madly in love with a young girl three years ago. We got married and began to live a wonderful life together.

We were the two happiest people in the world! And then, all of a sudden, she had a heart attack and died."

"I'm sorry to hear that," I said.

"Thank you," he said, and then went on. "I left our house the day she was buried. I have not gone back there since. It would make me too sad to return to that house."

I nodded. I could see why he might feel that way.

"But," he said, "it is lucky for me that we met today. I must ask you a favor."

"Of course," I said. For I wanted to help my unlucky old friend who was now so sad.

"Will you go to my old house and get some letters for me? They are very important. I cannot send a servant to get them. I can only ask someone that I trust very much."

"Thank you," I said, feeling proud that he put such trust in me.

"I cannot go myself. Nothing in the world could make me go into that house again."

My friend then told me exactly what he wanted me to do. First, I was to go to the house and find the gardener. He lived in a cottage just behind the big house. The gardener would unlock the big house for me. Then I was to go upstairs to my friend's bedroom.

"The door will be locked," he said, handing me a key. "Be careful with this key, for it is the only one for that bedroom. When you go in, you will see a large wooden desk. In the top drawer of the desk you will find the letters I need."

As I took the key from him, he put a hand on my arm. "One more thing. Please do not read the letters."

That hurt my feelings, and I told him so. Did he think I could not be trusted?

"Please forgive me," he said, tears coming to his eyes. "I have been so unhappy I seem to be forgetting my manners."

"That's all right," I said. "I understand how you must feel." Then I said goodbye and started off on the trip to his old house. The ride there was pleasant. It was a warm day and the sunshine was bright. As I rode along on my horse, I listened to the birds singing in the trees. When I got near the house, I took the letter for the gardener from my saddle bag. I was surprised to see that it had been sealed. That made me angry again. Could it be that my old friend really did not trust me after all?

I almost turned around and went back. But then I thought of how terrible my old friend had been feeling. He had been through so much sadness. Maybe he wasn't thinking clearly. Maybe he sealed the envelope by mistake. I decided not to let it bother me.

When I got very near the house, I was surprised again. The place was in very bad shape. A few of the windows were broken. The front gate hung from one hinge. The grass had not been mowed for a very long time. I tied my horse to a fence post and went to the gardener's cottage behind the big house. I knocked loudly. A minute later, an old man came to the door. I told him who I was and gave him the letter from my friend.

He opened it and read it. Then he stuffed it into his pocket and looked at me. "What do you want?" he said.

"You should know," I said. "You read the letter. I want to go into the big house."

A wild look came to the old man's face. "You mean you want to go into—into her room?"

"That is none of your business," I said.

"I'm sorry, sir," he said. "I only asked because no one has been in that room since—since her death. If you will just wait a few minutes, I will go to the room and see—"

He was beginning to make me angry. "What are you talking about?" I said. "Are you trying to trick me? I have the only key to that room." I held up the key my old friend had given me.

He nodded and turned toward the house. "Come this way," he said. "I will let you in."

I followed him to the house. As soon as he had unlocked the door, he turned and hurried back to his cottage. When I stepped into the house, I found myself in a wide hall. At the end of the hall was a set of stairs. When I reached their base, I stopped. The old stair steps did not look safe. As I climbed them slowly, they creaked as though they might give way.

At the top of the stairs I saw the door my friend had told me about. I tried the key in the lock and the door swung open. The room was so dark that I could hardly see. When I saw that the shutters on the windows were closed, I tried to open them. But they were stuck shut. Then I tried to pry them open with my sword— again without luck. Finally I gave up on that idea. I would have to make do in the dim light. I waited for my eyes to get used to the dark. Feeling the chill of the gloomy room, I wished I had brought a candle with me.

After a minute or so, I could see well enough to find the desk. I could also see that the bedroom was a mess. A chair lay on its side on the floor. The air in the room smelled stale. Dust clouds rose up as I crossed the floor. The sheets and covers were piled at the foot of the bed. There was a dent in the pillow, as though a head had just been resting there. A green door next to the bed was half open. It seemed to lead to another room.

I went to the desk and sat down on the chair in front of it. For a while I just sat there, still getting used to the dark. Then I opened the top drawer and looked in. Just as my friend had said, the letters were there. As I reached for them, I heard a strange sound behind me. A cold shiver went up my spine. I waited for a bit, but did not turn around. Then I reached again for the letters. As I took them from the drawer, I heard the sound of a deep breath in the room. There was no mistaking it.

I was so scared I jumped up from my chair, landing almost three feet away from it. My heart was beating madly as I turned to see who was there. A tall woman all dressed in white stood there staring at me. You had to be there to know what that sight was like. I had never known such horrible fear in all my life. I felt as if my blood had turned to ice water!

I have never believed in ghosts. Still, I suddenly felt a great fear of the dead. I simply stood there, my hands shaking. And then the woman began to speak. Her voice was sweet, but at the same time very sad. "Oh, sir," she said, "will you please do me a great favor?"

I wanted to speak to her, but no words came out when I opened my mouth.

She said, "Will you please help me? You can save me. I suffer so much—oh! how I suffer!"

I wanted to help her, but still I could not speak. So, I nodded to let her know I was willing to help. She handed me a fancy comb and said, "Please comb my hair. That will make me feel better. My hair must be combed. Look at my head. Oh! How I suffer!"

She sat down in the chair I had been sitting in. Her long, black hair reached almost to the floor. As I began combing it, I shivered at the way her hair felt. It was cold to my touch. Combing it was almost like handling snakes. Even today, the thought of it makes me shiver. I combed for a few minutes without saying a word. The strange woman did not speak, either. Then she suddenly stood up and turned to me.

"Thank you," she said, taking the comb away from me. Then she dashed into the other room, closing the green door behind her. As I stood there alone, my fears grew stronger. I began to shake. I could feel myself growing cold. At last I could stand it no longer. I needed light! I ran to the windows and pushed on the shutters with all my might. Finally, they flew open, and the room filled with light.

Without thinking, I ran to the green door and pulled at the knob. The door did not open right away. As I pulled at it, my fear grew. I had been afraid enough in the dark. Now, I was even more afraid in the light. I ran to the desk and grabbed the letters. Then I burst out the door and down the stairs. When I reached the front door, I kept right on running. I ran across the yard to where my horse was tied. In no time at all I untied and mounted him. How glad I was to be on my way home, riding as fast as I could! All the way there I kept thinking about that woman. Who was she? Where had she come from? Where had she gone?

When I got home, it was almost dark. I put my horse in the barn. By then I was feeling a little bit better. I began to wonder if I had been imagining things. Maybe I had fallen asleep while sitting at the desk. Maybe it was only some kind of awful dream. As I walked up to my house, I happened to look down at my coat. In a flash, my fear returned, stronger than ever. Strands of the woman's black hair were caught on a button. I pulled them off, one by one, and dropped them to the ground. Just as before, the strands of hair felt like snakes to me.

I did not go to my friend's house that night. I was too worn out. But that was not the only reason I stayed home. I was not ready to tell him what I had seen. It would take me a while to get my thoughts together. The next day I called on my friend, but he was not home. I went to see him again the day after that. Yet again, he was not home. I tried several more times, but he was never there. A week passed, and still I did not hear from him. It was then that I went to the police and told them my friend was missing. I also told them what happened at the old house.

The policemen checked the old house, but with no luck. They did not find him. They did not find the woman, either. In fact, there was nothing to show that the woman had ever been there. For weeks, the police looked everywhere for my friend. At last, they gave up trying. They could not find out where he went or how he vanished.

In the 56 years since that awful day, I have heard nothing more.

An Old Man

Is it possible to outwit old age? The vain old man in this story thinks he can stay alive forever. Could there be any truth in his theories?

"I KEEP FREE OF ILLNESS THROUGH CAREFUL LIVING."

An Old Man

All of the local newspapers had carried the following ad:

The new spa at Rondelis offers wonderful benefits. Visitors might want to stay for a long time, or even, perhaps, move in. Its waters are full of iron, which is known the world over for cleaning the blood. The mountains around the spa seem to have special qualities that can make a person live longer. The spa is in the middle of a forest of fir trees. For hundreds of years, people in this area have lived very long lives.

Thousands of people read that ad. Huge crowds came to the spa. One morning the doctor in charge of the springs was asked to call on a new visitor. It was a man named Daron, who had arrived a few days before. He had rented a charming villa on the edge of the forest. Daron was a little old man of 86, yet still quite healthy and active. He went to great trouble to hide his age.

After offering the doctor a seat, Daron started questioning him right away.

"Doctor, if I am in good health, it is because of careful living. Though I'm not very old, I have reached what might be called a respectable age. Yet I keep free of all illnesses through careful living. It is said that the climate here is very good for the health. I want to believe that. But before I settle down here, I must be sure. That is why I asked you to come here. I must insist that you give me certain information once a week.

"First, I wish to have a complete list of everyone over 80 years old who lives in the area. I also need a few details about each one. I would like to know what each one does for a living. I also want to know about their habits. Every time one of them dies, I would like to know about it. I want to know the exact cause of death and the circumstances."

Then he added, "I hope, Doctor, that we shall become good friends." He held out his wrinkled little hand. The doctor shook it and promised to do as the old man had asked.

Since his youth, Daron had always had a great fear of death. He had avoided nearly all the pleasures of this world because they were dangerous. Whenever anyone offered him a glass of wine, he would say no. "I value my life," he would say. He stressed the word *my* as if *his* life had more importance than anyone else's. The way he said it, no one ever argued with him about it.

For that matter, he *always* had a very special way of stressing the word *my*. He would say "my eyes, my legs, my arms, my hands," as if his body parts were not at all like other people's. When he said "my doctor," it was as if the doctor belonged to him and nobody else.

The truth was that Daron had never thought of other people as anything but puppets. He divided the human race into two classes. There were those he said hello to and those he did not say hello to. Both of these classes were equally unimportant in his eyes.

But when he got the list of people over 80, he took quite a sincere interest in them. There were 17 people of that age in the town. He did not wish to meet them, but he formed a very clear idea about each one. When the doctor joined him for dinner every Thursday, Daron spoke only of the people on the list.

"Well, Doctor," he would say. "How is Joseph Poinçot today? He was feeling a little ill last week." Then the doctor would give him the patient's bill of health. Daron would then give the doctor his ideas for changes in the diet and methods of treatment. It was his idea that *he* could use the same methods, if they worked with the others. Those 17 old people were Daron's experiments. And he learned a lot.

Then one evening the doctor said, "Rosalie Tournel has died."

"What of?" Daron asked.

"Of a chill," the doctor replied.

The little old man gave a sigh of relief. "She was too fat," he said. "She must have eaten too much. When I get to her age, I'll be more careful about my weight." The truth was that Daron was two years older than Rosalie Tournel. But he had told the doctor that he was only 70.

A few months later it was Henri Brissot's turn. The news made Daron very upset. This time it was a man who had died—and a very thin man. Not only that, he was within three months of

Daron's own age and careful about his health.

"What did he die of?" asked Daron, almost afraid to hear the answer.

"Of pleurisy."

The little old man clapped his dry hands with joy. "I told you so! I told you he had done something silly. You don't get pleurisy for nothing. He must have gone out for a breath of air after his dinner. Then he got a cold, and the cold went to his chest. Pleurisy! Why, that's an accident, not an illness. Only fools die of pleurisy."

Then he ate his dinner in a good mood, talking about those who were left. "There are only 15 of them now. But they are all healthy, aren't they? Life is like that. The weakest go first. People who live past 30 have a good chance of reaching 60. People who pass 60 often get to 80. Those who pass 80 nearly always live to be 100. That's because they are the fittest, toughest, and most careful of all."

Another two died that year. One died

of dysentery, and the other had a choking fit. Of course Daron decided that both of them had been careless.

"Dysentery is the disease of careless people. Doctor, you should have watched over his diet."

Then Daron decided that he knew what had caused the other man's choking fit. He said that the man had had a heart condition, but nobody had noticed it before.

Then one evening the doctor had to report that Paul Timonet had died. This man was a sort of mummy whom everyone expected to live to be 100. They had been hoping to use him to advertise the spa.

As usual Daron asked, "What did he die of?"

The doctor said, "Bless me, I really don't know."

"What do you mean, *you don't know*? A doctor always knows. Did he have something wrong with his liver or kidneys?"

"No, they were quite healthy."

"Did you check to see if his stomach was working right? A stroke is often caused by poor digestion, you know."

"There was no stroke."

Daron was puzzled. "Look," he said. "He must have died of *something*! What do you think it was?"

The doctor threw up his hands.

"I have no idea, no idea at all. He died because he died, that's all."

Then Daron asked, "Exactly how old was that one? I can't remember."

"He was 89."

And the little old man exclaimed, "Eighty-nine! So whatever it was, it wasn't old age. . . ."

Thinking About
the Stories

The Necklace

1. Look back at the illustration that introduces this story. What character or characters are pictured? What is happening in the scene? What clues does the picture give you about the time and place of the story?

2. Does the main character in this story have an internal conflict? Does a terrible decision have to be made? Explain the character's choices.

3. Good writing always has an effect on the reader. How did you feel when you finished reading this story? Were you surprised, horrified, amused, sad, touched, or inspired? What elements in the story made you feel that way?

The Umbrella

1. Which character in this story do you most admire? Why? Which character do you like the least?

2. What is the title of this story? Can you think of another good title?

3. Imagine that you have been asked to write a short review of this story. In one or two sentences, tell what the story is about and why someone would enjoy reading it.

The Specter

1. All the events in a story are arranged in a certain order, or sequence. Tell about one event from the beginning of this story, one from the middle, and one from the end. How are these events related?

2. The plot is the series of events that takes place in a story. Usually, story events are linked in some way. Can you name an event in this story that was the cause of a later event?

3. Are there friends or enemies in this story? Who are they? What forces do you think keep the friends together and the enemies apart?

An Old Man

1. All stories fit into one or more categories. Is this story serious or funny? Would you call it an adventure, a love story, or a mystery? Is it a character study? Or is it simply a picture the author has painted of a certain time and place? Explain your thinking.

2. Where does this story take place? Is there anything unusual about it? What effect does the place have on the characters?

3. Who is the main character in this story? Who are one or two of the minor characters? Describe each of these characters in one or two sentences.